The History of Peru

Peru

A Fascinating Guide

By
David Robbins

any kind are declared or implied. Readers acknowledge that the author is not engaging in the rendering of legal, financial, medical or professional advice. The content within this book has been derived from various sources. Please consult a licensed professional before attempting any techniques outlined in this book.

By reading this document, the reader agrees that under no circumstances is the author responsible for any losses, direct or indirect, that are incurred as a result of the use of information contained within this document, including, but not limited to, errors, omissions, or inaccuracies.

Table of contents

PRE-INCA PERU

Peru is somewhat unique in its region of the world, not only for its dramatic topography, diverse landscape and wildlife but also because of its pre-Columbian history. Unlike its neighbors and cousins in South America, it was home to an empire long before the colonial empires of Europe arrived.

Complex and storied, Peru's pre-Columbian days are thought to have started over twenty thousand years ago. Coming over from what is now Asia, historians and archeologists believe that Peru's first residents crossed over the Bering Strait to America.

Proof of cultures and tribes in what is now known as Peru has been found all over the country. Archaeologists have found hunting weapons and tools that date back to 11,000 B.C. inside caves in Junin, Lauricocha, Pachacamac and Telarmachay. These were thought to be from the first peoples who were nomadic and followed the migration of prey animals to survive. But that changed as people reached more fertile lands such as Kotosh and Huaca Prieta.

Having the means and the lands to settle down, many of Peru's early tribes switched from a nomadic to an agriculture-based society. Evidence of farming and cultivation tools along with signs of domestic animals signaled a dramatic shift in the early Peruvian lifestyles.

As tribes settled down into their new lifestyles and stopped traveling as much, their cultures naturally changed. They grew corn and cotton. Signs of advancement came with the knitting and quilting of wool, basketry and pottery.

With more abundant resources, Peruvians set up the first known city in the Americas. This came from an expansion into the Andes Mountains and the Pacific coastline. In the Supe Valley, about two hundred kilometers from what is known today as Lima, the city of Caral was founded.

More than one hundred and fifty acres large, Caral was the most ancient city in North, South and Central America. Historians and archaeologists believe that it was home to more than three thousand of the Norte Chico people. Among the very impressive findings at the ancient city were six pyramid-like structures, platform mounds made of stone and dirt, amphitheaters, temples, residential areas and even sunken circular plazas.

Caral is a marvel of the ancient world. It could proudly stand next to any of the cities of ancient Egypt, Mesopotamia, China and Egypt as an equal. UNESCO made it a world heritage site. Their quote on why they did so does the city and the Norte Chio people who inhabited it justice:

"The Sacred City of Caral-Supe reflects the rise of civilization in the Americas. As a fully developed socio-political state, it is remarkable for its complexity and its impact on developing settlements throughout the Supe Valley and beyond… The design of both the architectural and spatial components of the city is masterful, and the monumental platform mounds and recessed circular courts are powerful and influential expressions of a consolidated state."

The Norte Chico, with their capital city of Caral, was an advanced and complex Pre-Columbian society that generally lived in the Fortaleza, Pativilca and Supe River valleys. It's thought that they picked these areas for the land's ability to grow produce such as beans, squash, guava and sweet potatoes, plus proximity to the water where they could fish.

With an intricate form of government, a clear gift in architecture (especially when it came to infrastructure and monuments), cotton- and food-based economy, and an involved religion including multiple deities and supernatural beliefs, the Norte Chico should be considered close to or on the same level as the Ancient Egyptians and Chinese. It's only recently that their achievements have been documented by historians and archaeologists.

Along with the Norte Chico, there was a wide variety of Andean tribes in pre-Columbian Peru. They would come and go. Some were absorbed by larger tribes. Others fell victim to flooding, earthquakes or other natural disasters. What stands out is how advanced they were compared to indigenous people in the surrounding continent.

Tribes and societies in Pre-Columbian Peru made much advancement and they weren't limited to those comparable to other natives in South America, such as cultivation of livestock, wool and agriculture. Archaeologists have found proof of pottery, ceramics, knitting and even metal working (gold and silver). By 700 B.C. the ingredients for the dominant Pre-Columbian empire were in place. The Incas were coming.

THE INCA EMPIRE

The Inca Empire was the largest in the Pre-Columbian Americas. From 1438 to 1533, the Incas dominated a huge swath of Southwestern South America, encompassing Peru, northwest Argentina, western and south central Bolivia, southwest Ecuador and parts of Chile. Their civilization was remarkably advanced while at the same time wholly unique. That was especially true when compared to other civilizations of the Old World.

The Inca Empire both marked the height of and the end of the Andean tribes of Peru. Its brilliance and downfall marked the end of thousands of years of indigenous Andean culture in the region. So where did it start?

Two large Andean Empires pre-dated the Incas. The first was the Tiwanaku who lasted from 300- 1100 AD. Located in what is now modern day Western Bolivia, the Tiwanaku were one of the most important Andean civilizations. Its influence can be felt even today in Peru and Bolivia.

The Tiwanaku chose to settle in land ripe for agriculture. In fact, the land supported large-scale farming that could feed their empire, including Tiwanaku, their urban capital city of the same name. Another notable feature was the fact that they were multicultural. People from different religions, racial backgrounds and tribes were drawn there, not only for the abundant food but also because of the monuments and religious festivals.

In fact, Tiwanaku was a destination to which people traveled from hundreds of kilometers away to pray to and visit monuments. Pilgrims in long llama caravans brought trade, new ideas and new foods with them. They carried offerings to their gods and prayers from family back home.

No one knows for sure why the Tiwanaku's vibrant civilization collapsed. Scientists, historians and archaeologists have competing theories as to why this Inca precursor disappeared. One of the leading theories is severe drought. Being so dependent on farming and produce left them vulnerable to drastic changes in weather. Without abundant food, people left, people died and the civilization's power and prestige went with them.

Others believe that the social dynamics of Tiwanaku collapsed, leading to the empire's demise. What does that mean? Those who support this theory believe that social unrest, perhaps in concert with a drought and food shortages, caused irreparable damage to the society.

There's physical archaeological evidence that the capital was destroyed on purpose. Damage to the remnants of structures that survived through the centuries show intentional wounds. Great monuments and gates are thought to have been tipped over by humans not the ravages of time. Some buildings and complexes show signs of being burned. Food jars were smashed. This destruction was thought to immediately pre-date complete abandonment of the city and dissolution of the empire.

After the Tiwanaku Empire collapsed, there's evidence that its people moved southwards in a mass migration. This directly affected the Mapuche society in Chile as they had to deal with this influx of people fleeing drought. Even today, many Chileans are some of the last remnants of this once great progressive empire, those vestiges found hidden in their blood, their DNA.

The other major Andean Empire that pre-dates the Incas was the Wari. The Wari called the central highlands of Peru home. They co-existed with the Tiwanaku, lasting from about 600 A.D. to 1100 A.D. In fact, some believe that they actually came directly from the great highly religious empire.

There is a debate over whether or not the Wari were actually an empire. Many believe they were simply a very large society made of economic Wari centers. Detractors also thought that there wasn't strong central leadership in a capital city, disqualifying it from being called an empire.

Despite doubts about whether the Wari was an empire or not, new evidence suggests that it indeed was. First, a vast network of roads in the region that connected provincial cities and trade points was discovered. Also, architecture and monuments were found, all sharing the same styles and characteristics, suggesting they were built by the same people. Then came the 2003 discovery of a pristine, undisturbed tomb.

El Castillo de Huarmey, an imperial tomb, contained a lot of convincing evidence of Wari wealth and the political powers that came with it. Three women of royalty were found entombed there along with six servants or family members, a practice found in empires all over the world throughout history.

The best comparison of the relationship with the Wari and Tiwanaku, is the West and the Soviet Union during the Cold War. Both empires were large, powerful and formidable, but unlike the sides during the Cold War, both got their power and wealth from having plenty of resources. A lack of cause and a more ancient form of mutually assured destruction stopped them from ever formally going to war.

It's perhaps fitting that the Wari and Tiwanaku existed at the same time because they both collapsed around the same time. Not only that, their reasons for collapse are thought to be the same: environmental factors and social unrest.

Knowing about the empires predating the Inca is important. The Inca Empire shared many of the same characteristic and cultural practices, and many of the people of the long past civilizations are later folded into the Inca. Some of the ills of those societies are later found in the empire that followed them.

German geographer Carl Troll proposed a theory about what led to the rise of the Inca after the fall of the Wari and Tiwanaku. He thought there were three factors that facilitated the empire's rise: a staple food, a reliable form of transport and technology.

Not only were the empires before the Inca important. They paved the road for the great empire to come. But it wasn't the only factor that led to its development. One of the biggest reasons is actually a lot more humble and is found in the form of a food, Chuno.

Chuno was made from a frost-resistant form of potato. Those potatoes were naturally freeze dried in low nighttime temperatures in the Andes. Then the potatoes were left out in the sun completing a five-day process that produced a hearty form of cheap food that made it ideal for the everyday person in Peru.

Llamas provided a stable form of transportation among other uses in the Andean region. The distribution of the pack animal was dense in the area, not only allowing individuals to travel much longer distances then they can on foot, but also allowing traders and farmers to transport their produce and goods all around Peru.

Lastly, Carl Troll believed that irrigation technology led to the Inca's rise and allowed them to stay in power. Greatly aiding farming, irrigation technology was necessary to support a large population, and the Incas were well-versed in the methods and techniques to do so.

At first, the Incas were a pastoral tribe of peoples from the Cusco region of Peru. Pastoral tribes were nomadic and mainly moved with whatever animals or livestock they raise. For example if a tribe raised cattle, if they were pastoral, they'd move with the cattle as the creatures find new places to graze.

According to the Inca's oral history, the origin of the Incas started with a mythological story. This story involved three caves. The center cave was called Qhapaq T'uqu. On either side of Qhapaq T'uqu were two other caves, Mara T'uqu and Sutiq T'uqu.

One day, out of the center cave (Qhapaq T'uqu) emerged eight people. There were four brothers and four sisters. The brothers were: Ayar Manco, Ayar Cachi, Ayar Awqa and Ayar Uchu. The sisters were: Mama Ocllo, Mama Huaco, Mama Raua and Mama Qura. The side caves (Mara T'uqu and Sutiq T'uqu) produced other ancestors of the numerous Inca clans.

Out of the brothers, Ayar Manco was thought to be the most important. Carrying a magic staff made of gold, he decided wherever he planted that staff would be where his new people would live. The brothers embarked on a long trip to find where Ayar Manco wanted to start their civilization. Not all of them made it to the finish line.

Ayar Cachi spent the trip bragging to his brothers about how strong he was. From all accounts through the Inca oral history, he couldn't really shut up about it. So his brothers, sick of hearing it, decided to play a prank on him. He was tricked into returning to Qhapa T'uqu where there was a sacred llama. Not being the smartest brother, he returned to that center cave and his brothers made it cave in, trapping him there.

Another one of the brothers, Ayar Uchu, also didn't continue to the end of his brother's quest. He decided to stay behind and stand atop the caves. Instantly he turned to stone and spent eternity looking over and watching out for the Inca people. For his heroic sacrifice, he was worshiped and people made the pilgrimage to see him.

Not a fan of the journey and that his brothers were breaking off in other directions, one of the brothers decided to go his own way. That was Ayar Awqa. The loner of the group he left his siblings to their own fates and forged his own path.

With one brother trapped in a cave, the other turned to stone and another decided to take his own path, only Ayar Manco and his sisters remained as they continued his quest to find a homeland for the Inca people. Finally they reached their destination: Cusco.

Upon reaching what he determined would be his people's homeland, Ayar Manco stuck the shaft of his staff into the dirt of Cusco. The problem was, Cusco was already populated and the people there weren't willing to just hand over their home without a fight.

Unfortunately for those who lived in Cusco when Ayar Manco and his sisters arrived, one sister, Mama Huaco was an amazing warrior. When the natives attacked, by simply using one of her bolas they were struck and killed instantly. This prowess and deadly skill scared the other natives so much they immediately surrendered and/or fled.

With his dominance over Cusco cemented, Ayar Manco became known as Manco Capac. Manco Capac would be regarded as the founder of the Inca people. Alongside his sisters they built the first Incan homes with their own hands. They constructed the first city in the Cusco Valley and laid the first brick for an empire to come.

Like his brothers before him, Manco Capac eventually turned to stone. Later generations would come to visit and revere him. His son, Sinchi Roca became the second emperor of the Inca.

While the facts in the Inca origin story can certainly be questioned, the story lived on. It brought their people pride that from nothing, literally stepping out of a cave in which they lived, this group of siblings founded the biggest and most influential empire in the Americas.

Under Manco Capac, the first Incan city, the Kingdom of Cusco, was built. It was the base for the Inca people and where their expansion radiated out of. That started with a leader named Pachacuti- Cusi Yupanqui, a Sapa Inca (paramount leader).

A Sapa Inca was the absolute undisputed leader and ruler of the Inca Empire. With complete control and power over the military, politics, social issues and the economy this was much more than just a ceremonial or figure head position. Sapa Incas were very active.

Sapa Incas were in charge of many things including the construction of infrastructure, temples and monuments. They ordered impressive feats of engineering like the Sacsayhuaman, a fortress that took half a century to complete. Under their commands, vast networks or roads were built, linking the cities and villages of the empire. Hanging bridges and tambos were erected to aid in traversing the harsh mountain environment of the Andes. And, unlike many leaders of empires throughout history, Sapa Incas appeared to have been good about making sure all the things they had built were very well cared for and maintained. They understood that keeping things in great shape kept them functioning properly.

Similar to other rulers in empires of the ancient world and unfortunately also the modern, the Sapa Inca was seen as holy and in some cases, deities. Seen as the living embodiment of the sun, the Sapa Inca was also regarded as all Incas' father. They also insisted that their people keep up religious practices, worshiping the gods that look over them all.

Part of a Sapa Inca being seen as divine came from his appearance, which was of the utmost importance. Often seen sitting on his golden throne, the Sapa Inca was clad in an ornate headband or military helmet. He carried a scepter and/or a feathered pike. It was also crucial that he never wore the same clothes twice. For example in religious ceremonies he wore something completely different than the every day. An assembly line of cloths, wool and fabric garments came in and out of their palaces.

Beyond overseeing the construction of an empire, the Sapa Inca had a variety of other duties. He organized the empire's calendar and sent inspectors to check up on civil servants. Those civil servants' loyalty and efficiency were observed and reported back to the ruler. Officials had to be sent out to collect taxes. Trusted governors were appointed and placed in strategic positions throughout the empire.

But the Sapa Inca not only gave orders and collected taxes, there was a more progressive aspect to them. Also known as Huaccha Khoyaq ("Lover and Benefactor of the Poor"), it was the Sapa Inca's responsibility to make sure the impoverished were looked after. He was in charge of the distributions of food, especially during droughts or other disasters. He held great state-sponsored religious feasts and even made sure that work was provided for the unemployed Inca.

What happened after a Sapa Inca died or stepped down was wholly unique to the Inca. Instead of just inheriting everything their father had before them, the eldest son and next Sapa Inca started fresh. He was to build his own royal clan or panaka. The previous Sapa Inca's (his father's) land, houses riches and wealth was actually passed down to his other children who didn't succeed him.

Sapa Inca Pachacuti-Cusi Yupanqui, translated to "earth shaker," started the Inca age of expansion in 1438. He and his son after him shaped the Inca Empire as we know it today and conquered almost all of modern day Peru.

Pachacuti-Cusi Yupanqui was the ninth Sapa Inca. Under his reign, the Inca went from a modest society to a true empire that would defeat and rule over their rival the Chimu. Within three generations of the expansion he started, the vast majority of Southwestern South America was under Inca control.

One of the first things Sapa Inca Pachacuti-Cusi Yupanqui did was reform Cusco into Tahuantinsuyu. That was made up of a centralized government, with, of course, the Inca at the head of the table and on the throne. Under the Inca were four provinces with governments of their own led by strong rulers: Antisuyu in the North East, Chinchasuyu in the North West, Kuntisuyu in the South West and Quallasuyu in the South East.

Careful to make sure that none of the provincial governments turned against the Inca, Pachacuti-Cusi

Yupanqui kept and embedded a network of spies in the regions. He also sent spies and scouts to unaffiliated villages and cities to come back and report on their military strength, economic strength, political system and more. Armed with that info he could fashion an offer of the proper gifts and incentives to join the empire.

Sapa Inca Pachacuti- Cusi Yupanqui's offers for other cities and villages to join the Inca and the Tahuantinsuyu weren't really offers. They were more like polite demands. Because the rulers in these unaffiliated regions knew that if they did not give in and join, they will be conquered by a far superior military. Once that region was conquered, its leaders were executed and their children were forced to come to Cusco City to learn about Inca politics and administration. Armed with the knowledge they gained as captives, these children of rulers and royalty would return home and implement those ideas.

Determined not to breed discontent and rebellion, the children of conquered rulers were also forced to wed into royal families in the Tahuantinsuyu. That way they would have blood ties to the Inca Empire, making it much harder to rebel. Such calculated political moves and military might is what allowed Sapa Inca Pachacuti- Cusi Yupaqui to build a true empire.

Sapa Inca Pachacuti- Cusi Yupanqui's son, Tupac Inca Yupanqui, led his father's armies. Tupac Inca Yupanqui started a campaign to conquer north of the Empire in 1463. That only continued after his father's death in 1471. Tupac's ambition led to a clash with their only real competition in the region, the Kingdom of Chimor.

The Kingdom of Chimor on Peru's northern coast was expanding at the same time as the Inca. That was halted as they ran into those Inca and a war broke out. It was a fairly one-sided war. Armies led by Tupac Inca Yupanqui, son of the earth breaker, conquered the Chimor and added them to the Empire. By the end of that war, the Inca Empire expanded into Ecuador and Columbia. When Tupac Inca Yupanqui passed away, a war hero and great Sapa Inca, his son, Huayna Capac, took over just as his father did before him.

Expansion of the Inca Empire continued. Their lands included all of the sizable country of Peru, western and South Central Bolivia and the majority of Ecuador as well as Chile. And it didn't stop there. Corners of Argentina and Columbia were added as well during Huayan Capac's reign. Neither he nor his empire could see what storm was brewing on the horizon as the Sapa Inca approached the end of his life.

FALL OF THE INCA

From 1524-1526 a Spanish explorer, Francisco Pizarro, was in the midst of exploring South America. Looking for gold and silver, he was led to many regions across the continent including the southern half. With him and his men came the ravages of smallpox, a virus of which the Inca and other South Americans had no immunity.

Sapa Inca Huayan Capac heard word of these strange people from a strange land in South America exploring the borders of his empire. So, he and a contingent of Incas went to investigate for themselves. Though he never actually got to meet them, he met the virus they brought with them, smallpox. It was a fatal encounter. Huayan Capac died from smallpox in 1527. Shortly after, his eldest son, Ninan Cuyochi, fell victim as well.

With Sapa Inca Huayan Capac dead as well as his eldest son, the Inca Empire as faced with a situation they never encountered before. No one knew who the next Sapa Inca was rightfully. There weren't even any clear rules of succession to fall back on. It all came down to his two remaining sons with different mothers, Atahualpa and Huascar.

The factor of the mothers of the two sons of Huayan Capac was a central issue in the dispute that turned into a war. Huascar was supported by the Inca nobility, religious figures and politicians mostly because of his heritage. He was seen as the "pure" Inca since his mother, Chincha Ocllo, and his father were actually siblings. So their lineage could not be brought into question. But he had a bad temper, was notoriously disrespectful, and didn't seem to care about customs and laws.

Atahualpa, on the other, hand was born to a mother who was not in the royal family, though she came from nobility. To make matters worse for him, his mother was the daughter of a tribe that stood against the Inca before in the North. Because of that fact though, he had a lot of support in the Northern reaches of the empire. Unlike his half brother he had an even temper, carried himself with dignity and was seen to be much smarter.

Unfortunately for Atahualpa and the Inca Empire, the calmer, wiser son of Huyan Capac was seen as illegitimate. Huascar was given the throne, but it went further than that. Angered that Atahualpa was a brother he saw as a bastard, Huascar wanted strip him of his lands and force him to pay homage to the new Sapa Inca.

Incans soon realized the gravity of their mistake when Huascar started demanding allegiance and tributes.

Not wanting to cause waves or further any hostilities, Atahualpa sent one of his most trusted men to Cusco with a large tribute of gold and silver for the new Sapa Inca. It was not meant with gratitude. Instead, Huascar was convinced it was all a ploy and his half brother was plotting a rebellion against him.

Huascar had some of Atahualpa's messengers killed before they could leave Cusco. Some of his brother's other men, trusted valued captains, were sent back home dressed as women as an ultimate insult. Enraged, Atahualpa declared war and the Inca Civil War began.

Knowing that around this time, a Spanish envoy was coming to meet Huascar, Atahualpa figured it would be a great opportunity to surprise and kill his half brother. He sent troops to Cusco to capture him. When he realizes that the meeting wasn't in the capital, he redirected his men to kill him.

Huascar got wind of the coming attack from his half brother. Very angry that his half brother would have the audacity to attack him, he prepared his troops. In response, Atahualpa prepared his own army of former imperial army officers and soldiers, mostly from the northern regions of the empire who swore loyalty to him. He gathered them in Quito.

Politicians, military officers and generals loyal to Atahualpa made Quito a new capital of the Northern Empire. More comfortable with an even-headed, wiser, less erratic leader who had the blood of a conquered king, they gathered to support him. Atahualpa declared himself the new Sapa Inca and Quito, the Inca Empire capital.

Huascar moved his army north. His target was Tumebamba, which his armies overtook in a surprise attack. Atahualpa was actually captured and it looked like the civil war was over. But what was an ongoing theme in this mess of a war, Huascar and his men botched it.

Drunk and celebrating their victory in the Civil War, Huascar's men made the major and costly mistake of letting a woman into their camp to see Atahualpa. She slipped him the necessary tools to free himself. That night he broke out of his restraints and rejoined his army.

Newly freed and having just been a stone's throw from death, Atahualpa was reinvigorated. He went to Quito to prepare a counter attack against Huascar's forces. Comprising mostly of military veterans and battle heartened warriors from the more dangerous Northern section of the empire, his army was formidable.

Atahualpa's superior army and tactics helped him move south, pushing back Huascar's forces. From 1531-1532, a series of battles waged across the empire. It culminated in a battle at Mochacaxa. It was a slaughter, and an important one because they captured Husacar's head general, Atoc.

Bolstered by the victory at Mochacaxa, Atahualpa moved south as fast as he could. In every following battle, his armies were victorious. When he reached the large, strategically important city of Cajamarca he was able to turn some of his half brother's men to his side. Those that wouldn't turn were first offered ways to join him peacefully. When that failed he used extreme violence, murdering an unknown but very large number of citizens. Those that survived instantly chose his side out of fear of meeting a similarly violent end.

It was becoming clear that Atahualpa was going to win the civil war. His armies kept pushing southward. Finally in 1532, Cusco and Huascar were captured. And the war ended. But as the brothers fought, a new more insidious and dangerous threat was spreading throughout the Inca Empire, the Spanish.

Spanish Explorer Francisco Pizarro and his brothers, Juan, Gonzalo and Hernando, were attracted to Peru by stories of riches and a wealthy South American empire. Curious and greedy they managed to get permission for an expedition from the Spanish Monarchy in 1529 and landed in the country in 1532.

It wasn't Francisco's first time in Peru, he'd visited there about five years prior. When he returned he found a much different Inca Empire. Ravaged by civil war and disease (the same smallpox he brought with him on his original expedition to the country), he saw a vulnerable empire. He took advantage and settled the first Spanish settlement in Peru. It was in the north of the country and was named "San Miguel de Piura."

The first Inca who saw and ran into Pizarro thought he and his men were gods, and for good reason. They came on large wooden ships, the like of which they'd never seen before. The Spanish had metal army and weaponry, like swords and pikes. In their arsenal they brought guns which were completely foreign to Peruvians at this time. Word got back to Atahualpa that the strange foreigners returned to the empire and had dug in roots.

In order to gain some more information on the strange foreigners on Inca land, Atahualpa sent a warrior named Cinquichara to gather more information on them and act as a translator since he knew Spanish. When Cinquichara returned, he brought with him reports that these strangers were not gods but very much just men. They ate like men, drank like men, fornicated like men and fought like men. There were no miracles performed and their numbers were small, less than two hundred.

Along with the news of how unremarkable the Spanish actually were, Cinquichara talked about how terrible they were. He told Atahualpa that they bound and enslaved native with shackles. And they took and killed whatever and whomever they wanted. His recommendation was to kill them. The plan he suggested was to burn them as they slept and trap them in their sleeping quarters, huts or tents.

Pizarro, knowing that he needed to open some kind of more direct communication with the Sapa Inca, sent one of his captains, Hernando de Soto, to meet with Atahuapla. Soto arrived at the meeting on a horse, of which Atahualpa had never seen before in his life, with a prepared message that preached the greatness of God and the conversion to Christianity. Predictably, it wasn't well received. But not being a knee jerk type of man, the leader of the Inca didn't respond violently.

In response to Pizarro's message, delivered by Hernando de Soto, Atahuapla said he'd meet with a talk to the Spaniard explorer, but only in person. So Pizarro met with the Sapa Inca. For his troubles he was told point blankly that the Inca did not trust him, they weren't happy with his treatment of natives and the fact that he and his men have been robbing, stealing and killing on his lands. Pizarro insisted that wasn't the case and left peacefully agreeing to meet again the next day in

Cajamarca. Atahuapla made a mistake and never should have let him leave his camp alive.

Fresh off the defeat of his brother, Atahuapla was in Cajamarca fasting in honor of his victory and the possible future of a once again united empire. Instead of coming himself, Pizarro once again sent captain Hernando de Soto as well as his brother, Hernando Pizarro. They said that they were emissaries of the Spanish king and didn't want any hostilities. Instead they offered their help. Not only would they give the Sapa Inca their services as military men and advisers, they would introduce them to Christianity. Not only that, they invited the Inca leader to Pizarro's camp in the Cajamarca Plaza where the explorer would apologize and explain their business in his country.

Sapa Inca Atahualpa agreed to meet the Pizarro in his camp after his fast ended. On seemingly friendly terms, Hernando de Soto put on a demonstration of horsemanship to impress the leader who marveled at the strange animal. In response, refreshments and hospitality was offered and all seemed well. But the Spanish had no plans to end this dispute peacefully.

The next morning, Pizarro set a trap and waited for Atahualpa to arrive and ambush him. In good faith, Atahuapla arrived with about six thousand unarmed followers and subjects. Those numbers did not deter the

Spaniards. After all, they were civilized men of God and they were still just savages. It's unknown exactly what sparked the coming confrontation, but many believe it was simple miscommunication. No matter what started it, the results are not in dispute.

The Spaniards opened up with a volley of gunfire, weapons that the Inca were not familiar with, especially their lethal power. The Incas, unarmed and not fighters were devastated by the volleys. Severely outnumbered and desperate to escape, the Spaniards kept moving forward, finding their way out of Cajamarca Plaza. That, combined with a Pizarro-led cavalry charge, led to more of a massacre then a battle. It's though that two thousand Inca died in this initial outburst.

Unfortunately for Atahualpa and his men in Cajamarca, the vast majority of his army and generals were back in the capital of Cusco. Still, the Inca tried to fight back. Though they certainly had the numbers, the Spanish weaponry was far more advanced than theirs. And the Spaniards also wore armor, which wasn't invulnerable but was much harder to penetrate then what amounted to Incan bare skin. The Incas almost made some inroads, targeting the Spaniards unarmored legs, but it was too little too late.

Atahualpa was captured and Pizarro and the Spaniards escaped. With the Sapa Inca as their prisoner, the Spanish held all the cards. They threatened to kill him if any of Atahualpa's generals tried to make a move to take him back and wipe out the foreigners. His men, who were loyal and loved him, did not dare to put their emperor in danger. Again, their naivety and honor put them at a disadvantage against the Spaniards.

More than anything, the Spaniards valued gold. Knowing that, Atahualpa and the Inca offered more gold than Pizarro could possibly carry or use in return for the release of the Sapa Inca. Though they would certainly go ahead and take the gold, the Spanish had no intention of releasing the Inca leader. They couldn't, the threat of his death was all that kept the peace at the moment.

There was much debate among the Spanish in Peru, South America and Spain about what to do with the Sapa Inca. After they received a very large amount of gold that was melted down to bars and sent back to Spain, the crown demanded that the Inca leader be killed and the capital seized. And that's exactly what happened.

Atahualpa agreed to be baptized and accept Jesus as his savior in return for not being burned at the stake as a heretic. That didn't help. On August 29, 1533, the great Atahualpa was garroted and murdered. Soon after,

Pizarro led an army of 500 Spaniards to Cusco and conquered it. Spain was officially in control of the Inca, achieved with less than a thousand men.

The fighting between the Inca and the Spanish did not die with Atahualpa. In fact, the exact opposite occurred. Rebellions and oppositions against Spanish rule raged in the once great empire. It took the Spanish forty years to finally squash all the Inca rebels and solidify their rule in one of the largest countries in South America.

Very good at wiping out native cultures, the Spanish went about almost completely destroying the Inca culture. So much information about the empire was lost to time and European savagery. Add to that the effect of European illness to the people and the Inca were almost wiped from the face of the Earth.

Today, many Peruvians are proud of their heritage. There's pride in once being a great empire rich in culture, both good and bad. Many identify much more with the long-dead Incas then the Spanish who spread their DNA across the region. And it showed that no matter how mighty, during the time of colonization, no country in South America was safe.

COLONIZATION

After the death of Atahualpa and the dissolution of the Inca Empire, Francisco Pizzaro was for all intents and purposes in charge of Peru--a name the Spanish gave their new colony. He installed Atahualpa's son Tupac Huallpa as a puppet Sapa Inca. There was a series of native uprisings before the charade was torn down and Pizarro was formally in charge of the country. He named Cusco as the capital of the Spanish colony.

Perhaps ironic or just karma coming back to bite Pizarro, the Spanish colony of Peru found itself embroiled in a civil war between conquistadors after taking advantage of a Inca Civil War to gain power. Pizarro was up against his rival conquistador, Diego de Almargo. It was a war that the Pizarro brothers won but at a very steep cost. In 1541, Francisco Pizarro was assassinated by a group led by Diego de Almargo's son.

Even with all the dysfunction in their new colony of Peru, Spain did not falter in its colonization of the entire country. The first step was establishing the city of Lima. In return for converting natives to Christianity, the Spanish demanded tributes from the Peruvian populace. A colonial land tenure system was set up and indigenous people were ordered to raise Old World livestock such as cattle, crops and chickens, for their new masters. Any resistance was often violently and/or lethally punished.

In 1542 the vice-royalty of Peru was born. It didn't just have authority of Peru but also modern day Columbia, Ecuador, Panama and Venezuela. The first obstacle they had to tackle was the relative chaos after the death of Francisco Pizarro.

Spain, seeing a need for stability and a guiding hand in Peru, sent Blasco Nunez Vela to be the first viceroy in 1544. But the drama after Francisco Pizarro's death wasn't over. His brother, Gonzalo Pizarro, killed Blasco Nunez Vela feeling that his family had the right to rule over the land they conquered. So the crown sent another viceroy, Pedro de la Gasca, who captured and killed the out-of-control Gonzalo.

With the Pizarros out of the way, Pedro de la Gasca and the Vice-royalty set their sights on building up the colony of Peru. While this great undertaking was underway behind the scenes, Incas were dying at alarming rates. Before the Spanish arrived there were about twelve million Incas in the country. By 1520, there were only about nine million. By 1620, there was less than one million. For once the mass death of a native population was not done on purpose by the Spanish. The diseases they brought with them absolutely destroyed the locals and the Vice-royalty had to deal with an abundance of death every day, all around the country.

Things in Peru really progressed under the leadership of Viceroy Francisco de Toledo, who was appointed in 1572. He squashed the last of the Incas in their lost city of Vilcabamba. Then he executed the last link to the Sapa Incas of old, Tupac Amaru I.

With the ugly business of completely erasing the Incas out of the way, Viceroy Francisco de Toledo proceeded to try and develop the colony economically. His plan was to do so by taking advantage of the country's silver mines in Potosi. He chose to use a program of forced native labor to work the mines and produce silver as fast as possible. This quickly shot Peru up to the top of the list of Spanish colonies as far as the wealth they produced for the crown and colonial empire.

Francisco de Toledo made Lima the capital city of Colonial Peru, replacing Cusco. It grew into, perhaps, the most powerful and wealthy city in South America, mainly because of how much silver passed through it before returning to Spain. That precious cargo had to pass through the city before going to Isthmus of Panama and back to Seville. Come the eighteenth century, Lima became the foothold of Spanish power in the continent and home to Spanish aristocracy outside of their homeland.

Things went relatively smoothly after the time of Francisco de Toledo. It wasn't all smooth sailing but for a couple hundred years, Spain kept a tight grip on the colony of Peru. Everything started a turn for the worse in the eighteenth century.

Spain's ironclad hold on their South American colonies started to falter. Colonies near and around Peru, like Argentina, Bolivia and Brazil, started to change and rebel against the crown. Some were lost. With Seville's attention on turmoil in Europe and their colonies, local elites in Peru, some native, started to test the waters of rebellion.

There were two major rebellions in eighteenth century Colonial Peru. The first was led by Juan Santos Atahualpa in 1742 in the Andean highland regions, Jauja and Tarma. The other came in 1780, in the highlands near Cusco, led by Tupac Amaru II. It was no coincidence that the leaders of both rebellions took names from a proud Peruvian Inca history.

Not a lot is known today about Juan Santos Atahualpa. But we do know that he was a native Peruvian who led an indigenous rebellion against the Spanish. It's thought his rebellion was formed less from political views than cosmic ones. He was said to believe that the Spanish conquest of the Inca Empire upset the cosmic balance of the universe.

Juan Santos Atahualpa started his rebellion in the jungles of Quisopango. Ready to start his movement, he first expelled all Spanish or people with Spanish blood from the region. They left along with blacks. As his revolution grew, the Spanish, eager to squash such an uprising, sent troops to pacify the natives. Those troops failed.

Bolstered and emboldened by his defeat of the Spanish, Juan Santos Atahualpa, kicked out all Spanish missionaries and holy men. The Christian church was not welcome in his lands. That was one offense too many for Spain and the Vice-royalty of Peru.

General Jose de Llamas was sent to Andean highland jungles to deal with and squash Juan Santos Atahualpa's rebellion. Even though he was a seasoned veteran, the general failed. His men, at a disadvantage in unfamiliar lands, thick jungle and against those who lived there their whole lives, lost battle after battle. Not able to defeat the rebels, the Vice-royalty decided to simply cage them in with a series of fortresses and contain it so it didn't spread. Juan Santos Atahualpa died sometime between 1755 and 1756. No one knows how or why.

Tupac Amaru II's rebellion led to him becoming one of the most famous heroes in Peruvian history. It was a rebellion boosted by the idea of the return of Inca culture and in response to the Spanish Bourbon Reforms. Even though it was one of many rebellions in the late eighteenth centuries, his was perhaps one of the most famous before the war for independence.

The Tupac Amaru rebellion began with the kidnapping and killing of the Tinta Corregidor/ Governor Antonio de Arriaga on November 4, 1780. After the abduction, which took place at a party in Tupac's hometown of Tinta, Antonio de Arriaga was forced to write a series of letters. Those letters consisted of requests to Tinta's treasurer to send him money and weapons. He was also made to write letters to other powerful people in the region, requesting their presence and a faux meeting of the most influential figures in the town of Tungasca.

On November 10, having outlived his usefulness, Governor Antonio de Arriega was executed in front of a gathering of natives, mesitzos (mixed heritage Peruvians) and Criollos. It was a show of power and a show of what the people of Peru could do to the power base if they joined and worked together.

Tupac Amaru II moved his rebellion towards Sangarara. He picked up more supporters along the way for local populaces, mostly consisting of natives, farmers and mesitzos. To counteract this rapidly growing rebellion, Spanish authorities in Cusco sent a force of about thirteen hundred men. But when the rebels arrived, they did so with an army of several thousand. They crushed the Spanish forces in Sangarara. It was not long until Tupac Amaru's rebellion controlled all of the Southern Peruvian Peninsula.

The Spanish were not about to let Tupac Amaru II's rebellion take over the colony. So they sent an army with the combined forces of the colonial military in Cartagena and Lima. Even with a rebellion forty to sixty thousand strong at that point, the rebels couldn't defeat the might Spanish army. After taking back Cusco, the Spaniards kept beating Tupac's armies on the battlefield and routing his forces through acts of diplomacy and amnesty for all who abandoned him and the movement.

On April 5, 1761, Tupac Amaru II was captures alongside his family. He met a grim end. After being tortured, he was forced to watch the execution of his wife and children. Then he was quartered, but the pulling of his limbs apart failed so he was beheaded.

In 1808, French conqueror Napoleon Bonaparte invaded the Iberian Peninsula (Spanish and Portuguese). Napoleon's forces captured the king, King Ferdinand VII.

That threw the whole Spanish Empire into disarray. Turmoil at home and the Constitution of Cadiz gave birth to two Creole rebellions in Peru. Both were defeated and somehow the Vice-royalty of Peru remained as the last major Spanish loyalist stronghold in the Spanish Colonial Empire.

THE FIGHT FOR INDEPENDENCE

Peru in the early nineteenth century was surrounded by turmoil. Their neighbors were embroiled in fights for independence against the Spanish made easier by the problems the empire faced in Europe. In Argentina, Jose de San Martin fought for an independent state. In Bolivia, Simon Bolivar made strides towards autonomy from Spain. These two revolutionary leaders turned their attention towards the large country bordering the Pacific and not only saw an opportunity to help fellow South Americans gain their independence but in doing so would help their own causes as having more Spanish controlled land near them was detrimental.

Jose de San Martin was a general of Spanish-Argentine descent. Born in Argentina he left his home at a young age to study in Spain. There, he not only received a formal Western education but also received a military education.

When in Spain, Jose de San Martin fought in the Peninsular War against Napoleon Bonaparte and France. Disillusioned and aching to help his true homeland's struggle for independence, he returned back to South

America. Arriving in Buenos Aires he offered his help against the Spanish and Spanish loyalists/royalists.

Jose de San Martin fought alongside the United Provinces of the Rio de la Plata. After leading the Army of the North and fighting in the pivotal Battle of San Lorenzo, San Martin set his sights on the Vice-royalty of Peru.

Before he could take on the Vice-royalty, Jose de San Martin had to organize an army to take on the difficult task, the Army of The Andes. He gathered them together in Cuyo, Argentina. Then they undertook a monumental task, the Crossing of the Andes.

The Crossing of the Andes proved to be one of the most important events in South American history but also an incredibly impressive feat. Jose de San Martin led the Army of the Andes and Chilean independence fighters, with four thousand men, in the morning of January 19, 1817 towards the Andes Mountains with a goal of reaching Chile. Smartly he split the force into two because one third of the men he left with died during the journey.

Despite heavy losses, the majority of Jose de San Martin's forces successfully crossed the Andes Mountain Range and reached Santiago, Chile on February 13, 1817. Most of the royalists left the region before he got there but about one thousand five hundred stayed behind to fight. That led to the pivotal Battle of Chacabuco.

In Chile, after victory in the Battle of Chacabuco, Jose de San Martin left Valparaiso in 1820 with a force of four thousand two hundred soldiers and a compliment of warships. He landed in Lima, Peru in 1821 and proclaimed that Peru was free in a famous speech addressing the capital. In well-known excerpt of the speech, he said, "... From this moment on, Peru is free and independent, by the general will of the people and the justice of its cause that God defends. Long live the homeland! Long live freedom! Long live our independence!"

Celebrated as a liberator, Jose de San Martin was named: "Protector of Peruvian Freedom," but the fight was not over. There were still loyalists in Peru who held fast to their beliefs in it remaining a Spanish colony.

With partial control of Lima, Peru solidified, Jose de San Martin entered a meeting with fellow South American freedom fighter Simon Bolivar on July 22, 1822. It was agreed that Bolivar would take over the fight for Peruvian independence.

Jose de San Martin, for all intents and purpose, retired. He left Peru, Argentina and South America for France in 1824. There, by all accounts, he never took part in any military actions or planning of politics as a whole.

His legacy would live, on not only in Peru but in Argentina and all of South America as well.

Born into wealth in Venezuela, Simon Bolivar was sent to Spain for an education, much like Jose de San Martin. Introduced to the concept of Enlightenment, a young teenage Bolivar was convinced that he needed to join in and aid in the fight for Independence in Spanish colonies in South America. So that is exactly what the young Bolivar did.

In 1808, knowing and taking advantage of Spain being distracted by the Peninsular War, Simon Bolivar chose New Grenada (Columbia and Panama, as well as parts of Costa Rico, Ecuador, Nicaragua, Peru, Brazil and Venezuela) as his first target in his fight for independence. After victory in the Battle of Boyaca in 1819, New Grenada was liberated.

Spain, not about to just let any of its colonies to fall to freedom fighters without a fight, sent a very large army to crush Simon Bolivar and his armies in New Grenada. After brutal fighting, Bolivar and his revolutionaries prevailed in the Battle of Caraboro in 1821, liberating his home country of Venezuela.

After the liberation of the country of his birth, Simon Bolivar moved on and continued his fight. He led his forces into Peru and won two important battles, the Battle of Bombona and the Battle of Pichincha. Then he moved onto to Quito on June 16, 1822.

Simon Bolivar met with Jose de San Martin and was officially put in charge of the task of completely liberating Peru. Named dictator in 1824, Bolivar's army met and defeated the Spanish once again at the Battle of Junin in August 1824.

The wars for independence effectively ended after the surrender of royalist forces in the stronghold of Real Felipe Fortress in 1826. Though there were uprisings in the years immediately following that, the formal fighting was over. Spanish rule had been overthrown and Peru was on the precipice of being born.

Simon Bolivar had a reputation as an almost superhuman liberator. Rarely ever losing a battle and having the Spanish's number, he moved like a tidal wave through South America, ousting colonialists and loyalists wherever he met them. British historian Robert Harvey was quoted as saying this about Simon Bolivar:

"Bolívar achievements in Peru had been as staggering as any in his career of a year, from holding a strip of the country's north coast while himself nearly moribund, he and Sucre had taken on and defeated an army of 18,000 men and secured a country the size of nearly all of Western Europe...the investment of

personal energy, the distances covered and the four army expeditions across supposedly impassable mountain ranges had qualified him for superhuman status...His stamina and military achievements put him at the forefront of the global heroes of history."

Unfortunately, Simon Bolivar was a great liberator but not known for being the most moral of leaders. His rule was often cited as cruel and unnecessarily strict. Not only people but institutions like churches had their purses raided by his government and armies to pay for their wars. Outside of South America, much like many revolutionaries in history, he was not seen as a great hero but instead as a brutal but effective revolutionary.

THE REPUBLIC OF PERU

Peru, having been established as an independent country, had a rough go of it in its early years. It got involved in territorial disputes with its neighboring countries. There was a failed attempt to join Bolivia in the Peru-Bolivian Confederation.

Bolivian General Andres de Santa Cruz created the Peru-Bolivian Confederation. Its founding led to a power struggle in the region. Chile and the Argentine Confederation stood against them. Various incidents sparked a war between the two sides resulting in the War of Confederation.

Several factors led to the War of Confederation. First came concern over the melding of Peru and Bolivia. Not only did it make for a very large entity in the region but also a very rich one that threatened to tip the balance of power unfairly in their direction over their neighbors. Argentina was very threatened by this as they too were a large, rich powerful country that did not want to lose any clout or influence.

Another leading factor of the war was competition. All sides wanted control of lucrative commercial routes on the Pacific coast/side of South America. This was especially true for Peru and Chile. Both valued these routes and were not willing to concede anything to the opposing side.

Predating the War of Confederation was the Tariff War. Former Peruvian president, General Felipe Salaverry, signed a Treaty of Friendship, Commerce and Navigation with Chile, in January 1835. But after President Salaverry was replaced by General Luis Orbegoso, the new president declared the treaty null and void, angering the Chileans. Peru raised its tariffs on Chilean wheat. In response, Chile raised tariffs on Peruvian sugar. It was not until an outside party, an ambassador/minister from Mexico, stepped in that the hostilities between the two countries cooled down. But they were not forgotten.

A civil war broke out in Chile from 1829 to 1830. As a result, the former Chilean President, General Ramon Freire y Serrano, was exiled to Lima. Showing their support for the ousted leader, the Peru-Bolivian Confederation funded a failed expedition for Freire to take back control from the now Chilean President Prieto. After his failures, Freire was captured but tensions between Chile and the Confederation started to escalate sharply.

After the failed Freire expedition, a very influential and powerful Chilean politician, Diego Portales, took it upon himself to go on the offensive rather than wait for Confederation interference in Chile's affairs. He appointed a Spanish sailor, Victorino Garrido, command of a small Chilean fleet. That fleet was ordered to raid a Confederate fleet, which made port at Callao. On August 21, 1836, Garrido led a silent attack that resulted in him capturing three Confederate ships: the Santa Cruz, Arequipeno and Peruviana.

Despite the grave offense of Garrido's raid, the Peru-Bolivian Confederation did not want to jump head first into war with Chile. Marshal Andres de Santa Cruz tried to solve the dispute via negotiation. The Chilean representative with whom he met had many demands. Most were reasonable and agreed to by the Confederation. But one was not. Chile demanded the dissolution of the Confederation itself. Not getting that one sticking point resolved, Chile declared war on December 28, 1836.

At first, Chile's allies Ecuador and Argentina wanted no part in the war. They wished to remain neutral and not get involved. But the Confederation and Marshal Andes de Santa Cruz forced their involvement, primarily because Santa Cruz outwardly supported the opposition to Argentine leader Juan Manuel de Rosas. Argentina declared war against the Peru-Bolivian Confederation on May 9, 1837.

Things started off very rocky for Chile. Other than the mistake they and their allies made throughout the war by fighting separately and not working together, the Chilean public did not support involvement in the conflict. Martial law was declared and the Chilean people grew angrier and more disgruntled at the Prieto government -- Diego Portales in particular.

On June 4, 1837, less than a month after Chile's allies joined the war, Colonel Jose Antonio Vidaurre captured Diego Portales. He then invaded the capital of Valpraiso, believing that since the public was so opposed to the war, they would support the bold move to ouster the government that got the country involved in it in the first place. Even though Vidaurre was defeated, Portales did not survive the crisis and was shot and killed. Portales became a martyr in Chile and greatly bolstered support for the war, especially since conspiracy theories circulated that Juan Manuel de Rosas supported the attempted coup and murder.

The War of the Confederation started on the seas. The Confederation prevailed in these first battles of the war, capturing Chilean ships and the ports of Caldera, Huasco, San Antonio and Talcahuano.

As they struggled in the naval battles, Chile planned a massive offensive that would in theory end the conflict with the Peru-Bolivian Confederation quickly. In September 1837, a Chilean expeditionary force of two thousand eight hundred men, under the command of Admiral Manuel Blanco Encalada went to Islay, Peru (Southern Peru), landing in October.

Admiral Manuel Blanco Encalada's forces occupied the city of Arequipa. But things there did not go well. Disease spread throughout the Chilean ranks, decimating them and their morale. As they tried to negotiate a way out, Marshal Andes de Santa Cruz's forces surrounded and blockaded the city. A siege started.

Surrounded, trapped and after losing a conflict with Confederation forces in nearby Paucarpata, Admiral Manuel Blanco Encalada was forced to negotiate a surrender. On November 17, 1817 Encalada signed the Treaty of Paucarpata. In it they agreed to withdraw all Chilean forces from Confederation owned lands and cancel all Peruvian debts to Chile. Naturally, the people and government of Chile were outraged when they heard the news.

When Admiral Manuel Blanco Encalada returned to Valpraiso with his remaining fleet and army, he was greeted as a traitor. He was thrown in jail along with his closest advisers. Though he would eventually be released, his actions were a huge blow to Chilean pride and their war effort.

Refusing to honor the Treaty of Paucarpata, Chile dispatched a fleet of five ships under the command of Robert Simpson to impede Peruvian commerce in the Pacific. They did so knowing it would spark an armed response. On January 12, 1838 the Chileans ran into a Confederation fleet near the port of Islay. Both sides claimed victory in the resulting battle but really it was a stalemate.

By mid-1838, Chile had gained the naval advantage. Propelled by their recent successes on the seas, they moved toward Lima. Though they were briefly hampered by small skirmishes with Confederation forces, they were finally able to lay siege to the Peruvian capital.

A battle broke out near Lima, the Battle of Portada de Guias. The Chileans won and took control of Lima, occupying the city until August 21, 1838. But they abandoned it after they heard that a Bolivian army, led by Marshal Andes de Santa Cruz, was approaching.

Over the course of the next year, Chile and the Peru-Bolivian Confederation would engage in a series of battles. The most notable were the Battle of Casma, Battle of Buin and the Battle of Yungay. They traded very costly victories as the tide of the war swung back and forth.

The end of the War of Confederation started with the defeat of Marshal Andes de Santa Cruz in the Battle of Yungay. Then, on August 25, 1839, Peruvian President General Agustin Gamarra officially declared the dissolution of the Peru-Bolivian Confederation. Gamarra tried a last-ditch effort to invade and combine Bolivia and Peru into one nation but was defeated.

Still angry after their defeat in the War of Confederation, Peru became embroiled in another war with Chile in 1879, the War of the Pacific. It started with a border dispute between Chile, Peru and Bolivia. Bolivia and Chile both claimed portions of the Atacama Desert.

In 1874, after years of dispute over the Atacama Desert that almost resulted in war, Chile and Bolivia agreed that Chile would surrender a southern portion of the desert and in return, Bolivia would not raise taxes on any of the Chilean companies that operated mines in the area. But in late 1878, Bolivian dictator Hilarion Daza raised those taxes going against the two countries' agreement.

Feeling that raising taxes nullified Bolivia and Chile's agreement in the Atacama Desert, Chile moved people and soldiers back into the region that they previously surrendered to the Bolivians. Outraged, Daza and Bolivia declared war on Chile.

At first Chile had no desire to go to war, they didn't respond to Bolivia's declaration of war and stayed quiet. That was until they got word that Peru secretly allied themselves once again with their Bolivian allies. The Chilean government felt like they had no choice but to declare war back on the two countries and the War on the Pacific started.

The decision to go to war was initially seen as foolish for the Chileans. Not only were they already embroiled in a conflict with Argentina at this time but the combined might of Peru and Bolivia far outnumbered Chile's forces. But after five years of fighting, once again, Chile came out on top over their enemies in Bolivia and Peru.

After two losing wars, Peru's relationship with Chile was seemingly permanently scarred. Even today, relations between the two countries, while not as bad as during the War of Confederation and War on the Pacific, is tense. Looking back it seemed to be the bad influence of Peru's ally Bolivia that led them to ruin in two disastrous fights that hurt Peruvian pride and people.

Fresh off another loss in the War on the Pacific, Peru needed to commit its time and resources to rebuilding its country. But first, the government needed to reach some sort of state of stability. That long road started in 1894.

At the time Andres Avelino Cacera was president of Peru. But he had many enemies among the government and people. One such enemy was Nicolas de Pierola. Pierola joined the Civil Party of Peru and joined a guerrilla effort to occupy the capital of Peru and ouster Cacera.

In 1895, Nicolas de Pierola became the President of Peru. He changed the landscape of the government, switching it from military rule to civilian rule. During his term, which lasted until 1899, reconstruction was the priority.

Nicolas de Pierola's government went about working on reforms in Peru. He started with fiscal reforms needed when the economy took a downfall after the war with Chile. The military, having been removed from the main position of power in the government also needed reforming. More religious freedoms were granted to the Peruvian people. Last but not least, civil reforms were unveiled all over the country.

The reign of Nicolas de Pierola and the leaders after him came to be referred to as the "Aristocratic Republic." It lasted until the 1920s. During this time, leadership of Peru was handled by the social elite instead of Generals or the military.

After Nicolas de Pierola the next pivotal leader in Peru was Augusto B Leguias. He had two terms. The first was from 1908-1912. His second, more famous term was from 1919-1930. That latter term became known as "The Eleventh."

The Eleventh was a time in Peruvian history when the United States of America became more involved in the country's affairs. They injected capital into Peru. Above every other class, the bourgeoisie were favored. That, combined with dependence on American and other foreign investments, bred anger among the Peruvian general populace.

During the second term of Augusto B Leguias, Peruvian exiles in Mexico joined together to found the APRA (American People's Revolutionary Alliance) in 1924. This Marxist group moved across the Americas, including Peru, spreading a message of more rights for workers and the average man over the ruling rich. It morphed and became more about political unity than people's rights.

In 1928, a former APRA member, Jose Carlos Mariategui, formed the Peruvian Socialist Party. In 1929 his Peruvian Socialist Party created the General Federation or Workers. Socially the feeling of change was in the air in Peru, but first there needed to be a band-aid applied to still open wounds with their longtime enemy Chile.

Also in 1929, Peru and Chile signed a final peace treaty. The Treaty of Lima returned regions taken by Chile during the War of the Pacific and the years after. This dipped their contentious relationship into an ice bath for a while, leaving both countries with their hands free to deal with issues in their own lands.

The early 1930s were marked with violence and repression in Peru. These were specifically targets at members of the APRA and the Peruvian Socialist Party. Tens of thousands of APRA members were imprisoned, tortured or murdered. This was in response to a growing nationalist and populist movement where the socialist party almost took control of the country.

World War II came around and like the rest of the world, Peru had to choose a side. They broke off all relationships with Germany and Japan and joined the Allied forces, though their participation and support was extremely limited. Many think their joining the Allies was only to be accepted into the United Nations. It was not so much the war that had a big impact on Peru during this time but what was going on at home politically.

Two ideologically opposed political leaders vied for control of Peru's future after World War II. The first was

Victor Raul Haya de la Torre. He was one of the founders of the APRA. The second was Jose Carlos Mariategui.

Despite their ideological differences, Victor Raul Haya de la Torre and Jose Carlos Mariategui joined forces in their common goal of stopping the military from retaking control of Peru. It wasn't difficult. Both of them founded parties that helped the common Peruvian and the social and economic problems that plagued their country. So putting aside their differing ideas of how to achieve the same goals was not hard.

Unfortunately, Jose Carlos Mariategui died young, but Victor Raul Haya de la Torre continued their work. He was elected twice. He successfully kept the military at bay during his time in office and he enacted some sweeping social changes that were loved by the people.

When Victor Raul Haya de la Torre's time in office was over his successor was President Bustamante y Rivero. He worked with the APRA at first to try and cement a democratic system in Peru in order to prevent the rise of military dictators in the country. But his presidency did not go as well as he and many in the country, including his supporters, would hope.

President Bustamante y Rivero's first challenge came from the former president. He and Victor Raul Haya de la Torre were at odds. They had a lot of disagreements, a fundamental one being installing some military personal in positions of power to appease them and keep a coup from occurring. Without the support of the former president, President Rivero, the support of the APRA was lost.

Minister Manuel A. Odria urged President Bustamante y Rivero, along with other right wing members of the government, to ban the APRA to outlaw it. They saw a threat and felt that the only way to deal with was to squash. This was especially true since the APRA had grown so influential they actually prevented the president from enacting reforms and laws he needed to be passed. President Bustamante y Rivero did not listen.

Seeing President Bustamante y Rivero too soft to deal with Peru's problems and the APRA, Minister Manuel A. Odria became General Manuel A Odria. The General led a military coup to overthrow the democratically elected government. On October 29, 1948, the military once again took power in Peru.

First on now President Manuel A. Odria's agenda was to come down hard on the APRA, which he did. That won him some friends in the military, oligarchy and upper classes of Peru, but he was not a dumb man. He also decided to implement a populist agenda that endeared him to the poor and common Peruvians.

President Manuel A Odria's term in office was full of contradictions. He cracked down on the APRA and socialists, but he was a populist. He restricted and took away some civil rights and fostered an atmosphere of corruption. The economy, however, thrived during his reign. He implemented popular social policies, but they were way more expensive than advisable.

Many Peruvians feared that President Manuel A. Odria's dictatorship wouldn't end until he died or someone overthrew him. Even though he was largely popular, those in the APRA and communist party feared him and tried to turn the public tide against him. Seeing the writing on the wall, President Odria decided to take action to improve his public image and legacy. He allowed elections.

As President Manuel A. Odria and Peru prepared for an election, an upstart politician started his career. Fernando Belaunde Terry submitted his application for candidacy with the National Front of Democratic Youth. His application for candidacy was denied. That did not deter him.

Fernando Belaunde Terry organized and led protests in Peru after his bid for candidacy was denied. A famous image of him holding a Peruvian flag was printed on the front page of the popular news magazine, Caretas, the next day. Overnight, the young man became a symbol of change. Though his candidacy was not granted and the Odria dictatorship favorite Manuel Prado Ugarteche won the election.

Undaunted by his earlier failure, Fernando Belaunde Terry once again bid for the presidency in 1962. This time around he had his own party that he founded, Accion Popular. After a very tight race he came in second place behind APRA founder Victor Raul Haya de la Torre. The problem was that no candidate, neither Belaunde nor Torre, got the amount of votes necessary for someone to be elected into office. So, Victor Raul Haya de la Torre worked out a deal with former President Odria (who came in third) to give the dictator another term while easing restrictions on the APRA. This did not come to pass.

Rampant allegations of election tampering and fraud squashed any deal between the APRA and Manuel A. Odria. The Peruvian military, led by Ricardo Perez Godoy, ousted President Manuel Prado Ugarteche and made a temporary government that ruled until new elections could be held in 1963. Finally, Fernando Belaunde Terry, not tainted by the scandal of the election one year earlier, was elected.

At this time in Latin American history, revolution and communism was rampant. Inspired by the Cuban

Revolution, revolutionaries in countries in Central and South America rose up and tried to take power. In Peru, the Revolutionary Left Movement or MIR was formed. They undertook an attempted insurrection but were crushed by 1965, though the MIR and social unrest in Peru would go on well into the 1990s.

In 1968, once again, military rule returned to Peru. This ongoing theme plagued the country throughout its relatively young history. This time it was General Juan Velasco Alvarado who overthrew President Fernando Belaunde Terry. The first phase of the Peruvian military's nationalist program soon got underway.

Under President Juan Velasco Alvarado, the country undertook a massive agrarian reform program. He also nationalized a lot of Peru's most profitable industries. These included fishing, petroleum companies mining firms and some banks.

President Juan Velasco Alvarado's time in charge was not without its problems. Many saw him as a bad due to mismanagement of money and Peru's funds. Human and civil rights deteriorated, as often the case with military dictatorships. Lastly, his own physical health didn't last. So in 1975 General Francisco Morales Bermudez took control.

General Francisco Morale Bermudez's time as president was seen in a better light than his predecessor. He instituted a second phase of military government reform. His relied more on conservative policies meant to restore Peru's economy, which seemed to always be in a constant state of flux throughout the twentieth century.

In 1979, Francisco Morale Bermudez presided over a Constitutional Assembly, organized by Victor Raul Haya de la Torre. The Constitutional Assembly's aim was to return control of the government to civilians and write a new constitution.

MODERN PERU

The 1980s brought change to Peru while also reintroducing some themes and faces from its recent past. In May 1980, former president Fernando Beluande Terry was once again elected into office. At the same time the drug cocaine rose into prominence in not only Peru but the world scene. Insurgent movements rose in the more rural areas of the country. And the MRTA (Tupac Amaru Revolutionary Movement) came into prominence and led to internal strife within the country.

Peru became the cocaine cultivation capital of the world. Its tropical climate made it ideal for farmers to grow coca, the key ingredient of cocaine. Supported by drug cartels and corrupt government officials, the country became the originator of the vast amount of cocaine on the planet, including famous drug hot spots such as Columbia and Mexico.

The widespread growing of cocaine, especially in jungle-covered mountainous regions of Peru, had multiple detrimental effects, not only on the country but the world. First, the money made from the growth and sale of the drug helped fund guerrilla groups like the Shining Path and MRTA. Not only that, the money also funded the Peruvian government's attempts to fight those groups.

It cannot be overstated the amount of money generated by the seemingly innocent coca plant. First used as an upper to chew on by the Inca, it later became used to make one of the most addictive and profitable substances on Earth. With that money came criminals, drug dealers and cartels. And in a country with a poverty rate as high as Peru, selling cocaine became far too profitable and easy to pass up.

Cocaine also got more outside governments involved in Peruvian affairs. Most notably of those were the United States and its CIA and DEA organizations. With the American war on drugs in full effect, Peru became a battleground against drug cartels that in some instances led them to fund guerrilla groups that world go on to commit all manner of atrocities in the war ravaged country of Peru in the 1980s and early 90s.

One of the most impactful results of the rise and boom of cocaine was the rise of the most powerful cartel leader in not only South America but up to that point in human history. Pablo Escobar funded his empire with Peruvian cocaine. Every crime he and his men committed, every murder, every bomb was all due to the coca plants of Peru.

As democratic elections returned to Peru in 1980, a far leftist group called The Shining Path refused to take part in or recognize the elections as legitimate. Their rampages in Peru started during the May 1980 election. Shining Path members burned ballot boxes in the town of Chuschi. Though that event received little coverage at the time and the offenders were caught and persecuted, it was the first of many revolutionary acts against the country's government.

Slowly over the course of the decade, the Shining Path's numbers grew. They found their greatest support among the populace in the Andean regions of Peru. Locals there felt disenfranchised and forgotten by the government in the country's bigger cities, like Lima, and the path offered representation for these forgotten Peruvians. It did not take long before their methods took a darker turn.

People who were thought to have done the people of the Andean regions wrong or got away with crimes were captured and put on public trials by the Shining Path. The sentences carried out were far from fair, often very brutal and included public executions. This didn't cast the group in a bad light in the eyes of the populace though, it only made them look stronger and attract more supporters.

As the Shining Path grew, their actions drew the attention of the Peruvian government. Not wanting to look weak or panicked, the government, led by President Belaunde refused to declare a state of emergency in the Andean regions the Path operated in. Many urged the president to take police or military action to squash the group and restore order. But Belaunde was wary of using the military if it wasn't completely necessary because of the years of military dictatorship from which the country just emerged.

President Fernando Belaunde Terry eventually had no choice. His hand was forced and he declared a state of emergency in 1981 in the Andean regions of Apurimac, Ayacucho and Huancavelica. The military was granted power to simply detain anyone they thought suspicious or suspect. Naturally, that did not go well.

Armed with a decree from the president to do what they needed to do to end the Shining Path, the military's actions got out of hand, and sometimes downright horrific. Countless innocent civilians in the Andean regions under the state of emergency were kidnapped, interrogated, tortured, raped and even killed. In response the Popular Guerrilla Army fought back against the military and police. Both sides carried out massacres and murders, some provoked, others not. It got so bad that the police and military in those places started wearing ski masks to hide their identities out of fear of reprisals against their families.

In some Andean regions, the military recruited and trained peasants and civilians. They formed them into groups called "rondas," or anti-rebel militias. These rondas were poorly equipped but were some of the most brutal soldiers in the conflict with the Shining Path.

One of the most infamous incidents in the war with the Shining Path happened in the town of Lucanamarca, which was a perfect example of the savagery during this terrible chapter in Peruvian history. A ronda in the town abducted a leader named Olegario Curitomay. After dragging him into the town square, the anti-rebel militia stabbed and stoned him to death in a horrific display for the public to see. In response, the Shining Path upped the ante. Shining Path members came to Lucanamarca, went door to door, and massacred dozens of innocent civilians. They used hatchets, knives and guns to kill men, women and even babies.

The Shining Path didn't limit their activities to rural Peru. They also operated in the major cities. Various terrorist methods were used in the capital of Lima. In 1983, the power plant was sabotaged causing a city-wide black out. A campaign of bombings broke out, killing military, police, politicians and civilians.

At its height, the Shining Path controlled most of the country side in South and Central Peru. They also had a very large presence in the outskirts of Lima. They did not believe that human rights or decency had any part in what they saw as a just fight. Disgusted by all the bombings, assassinations and killings, a majority of the Peruvian public demanded a response and end to all the violence. So the government took action.

At first the government's responses to the Shining Path were not effective. Since their rondas and military often committed worse atrocities than the subversive group, the public saw the Shining Path in controlled areas as the lesser of two evils -- and often their operations were unsuccessful. That was until they captured the famed leader Abimael Guzman. The movement collapsed soon after.

It's thought that the Shining Path was responsible for the death and or disappearance of an estimated thirty-one thousand three hundred and thirty-one people. That's roughly one half of the victims who were lost. The government was thought to be responsible for one third of the total number and rondas and other guerrilla groups killed the rest.

Condemned by countries such as the United States, Japan, Peru and the European Union, the Shining Path's legacy is one of brutality and terrorism. Though it had a brief resurgence in the twenty-first century, the movement is remembered as one of the most reprehensible in modern human history.

The much smaller MRTA was another radical leftist group that would be designated terrorists during the 1980s. Named after the old Inca Sapa Inca, the group's goal was to inspire leftists all over Peru to rise up and force change to a government that they didn't believe properly represented the people.

The MRTA's actions started when they robbed a bank in La Victoria, Lima in 1982. It was to fund the movement and the operations to come. Like the Shining Path they weren't at first seen as a major threat or problem.

Their activities were less extensive then the Shining Path for several reasons. One, they didn't have the same numbers or support. Two, Peru's counter-terrorism efforts successfully kept them at bay. And three, they often found themselves at odds and fighting other revolutionary groups such as the aforementioned Shining Path.

On July 6, 1992 MRTA members raided the town of Jaen in Peru. They were ousted after an intense shootout, but a police officer was famously killed in the fighting sparking outrage. It was followed up by them invading the Japanese Ambassador's Home in Lima, during December 1996. Seventy-two hostages were taken and held for four months until the hostages were saved and all the MRTA fighters who took part were killed.

As so much internal problems took place in Peru with terrorist groups and guerrilla armies, President Fernando Belaunde Terry did his best to do good work through government. One of his first actions was to return newspapers that were seized by the military dictatorship of his predecessors back to their rightful owners. Free speech was returned to Peru. He also reversed many of the agrarian reforms instituted by Velasco. Plus, he addressed the country's relationship with the United States.

When the 1990s rolled around, most of the horror of the conflict with the Shining Path had passed but hadn't been fully dealt with. With terrorism concerns and worries about the economy, a relatively unknown mathematician turned politician, Alberto Fujimori, was elected president in 1990.

Alberto Fujimori's first measure was to drastically cut the out-of-control inflation in Peru. It devalued the currency, made thousands of public companies privatized and over three hundred thousand jobs were lost. The poverty rate did not change, it stayed somewhere around fifty percent.

Next, Fujimori broke apart congress in April 1992. He did it so he would have total and absolute control of Peru. Then he abolished the constitution. Of course, such drastic measures were not received lightly by the public or his enemies.

Alberto Fujimori fought to finish off the Shining Path. For the most part he was successful in doing so until atrocities were committed by his Peruvian forces and the insurgents they were fighting.

The Barrios Altos Massacre took place on November 3, 1991 in the Barrios Altas neighborhood in Lima, Peru. Fifteen civilians were killed in an action by the Grupo Colina. Consisting of Peruvian Armed Forces personnel, the government was held responsible for the slaughter. To make matters worse for Alberto Fujimori, one of the victims was an eight-year-old child who was definitely not a member of the Shining Path as his government claimed all the victims were.

The La Cantuta Massacre took place on July 18, 1992 at Lima's La Cantuta University. A professor and nine students were abducted, tortured and killed by a Peruvian military death squad. It was in response to a Shining Path bombing in Tarata that killed forty people. Desperate to make people answer for that terrorist attack, Fujimori's military committed another atrocity.

Alberto Fujimori tried to run for a third term in office in 2000. He won but the win was tainted by scandal. His right hand man, Vladmiro Montesiros, was caught on TV bribing a politician to change sides to Fujimori's. A subsequent investigation found that Montesiros was in the middle of a vast web of corruption and drug trafficking that was connected to the President. With drawing from a forced new election, Alberto Fujimori was finally out of power in Peru.

For once, a brutal Peruvian dictator did not escape justice. Alberto Fujimori, convicted in multiple countries for his litany of human rights abuses was imprisoned. Despite drama involving extradition and fights for pardons, he remains in prison today.

The healing in Peru started with the involvement of the Truth and Reconciliation Commission (CVR). The commission investigated and put in perspective the cost in human lives during Fujimori's reign, the terror of the Shining Path, and the military dictatorships that have dominated Peruvian history. In the best of circumstances, hopefully, seeing the atrocities in concrete numbers will help prevent such crimes from ever happening again. And those who committed such widespread human rights abuses have mostly been punished.

Peru is a beautiful country with a diverse environment including snow-capped mountains, pristine Pacific beaches and vast jungles. It carries with it a complicated history starting with the proud Incas, but it also faced its fair share of darkness with military dictatorships, wars against colonial powers and the fight against and with terrorist groups.

The future, however, looks bright for Peru. The economy is more stable today, along with the government. Those grim days of the Shining Path and government sponsored paramilitary groups have passed. Relationships with its neighbors, which have not always been positive, have improved. While far from perfect, this jewel in South America can and will see a brighter future.

SOURCES

https://en.wikipedia.org/wiki/History_of_Peru

https://www.chimuadventures.com/blog/2016/10/history-of-peru/

https://www.ancient-origins.net/ancient-places-americas/5000-year-old-pyramid-city-caral-002016

https://www.voyagesphotosmanu.com/peru_world_war_II_and_after.html

https://www.globalsecurity.org/military/ops/war-of-the-pacific.htm

https://www.livescience.com/41346-the-incas-history-of-andean-empire.html

https://www.history.com/topics/south-america/inca

https://www.ancient.eu/Inca_Civilization/

http://www.ushistory.org/civ/11c.asp

https://www.oxfordbibliographies.com/view/document
/obo-9780199766581/obo-9780199766581-0189.xml

http://motherearthtravel.com/history/peru/history-
5.htm

https://en.wikipedia.org/wiki/Shining_Path

https://perureports.com/shining-path/

https://www.britannica.com/topic/Peruvian-Bolivian-
Confederation

https://www.encyclopedia.com/humanities/encyclopedi
as-almanacs-transcripts-and-maps/war-peru-bolivia-
confederation

https://www.britannica.com/biography/Alberto-Fujimori

https://trialinternational.org/latest-post/alberto-fujimori/

Made in the USA
Coppell, TX
19 October 2022

84940196R00049